CHILTERN
ROUND
WALKS

Chiltern Round Walks

V. B. BURDEN

SPURBOOKS LIMITED

Published by:
SPURBOOKS LIMITED
1 Station Road
Bourne End
Buckinghamshire

I S B N 0 902875 63 9

Printed by Maund & Irvine Ltd., Tring, Herts.

Contents

(11) Seer Green.
   A journey through Quaker country —
   10½ miles

(12) Wendover.
   Climbing up to Boddington Banks —
   6 miles

ACKNOWLEDGEMENT
Acknowledgement is made to the *Bucks Examiner* and *Chiltern Life* for kindly allowing the use of some material previously printed by them.

INTRODUCTION

Give me the clear blue sky over my head, and the green turf beneath my feet. . . .   HAZLITT

THIS IS a further selection of walks, a sequel to *Round Walks West of London*. They range roughly from 4 to 10 miles. Being circular excursions they may, of course, be picked up at any point en route, but at the given starting point parking space is available, and in most cases is covered by public transport as well, though the latter becomes increasingly sparse.

However, the footpaths west of London are most certainly not sparse. They are numerous, clearly signposted and way-marked, excellently cared for and just waiting to be explored. They lead through some of the loveliest English countryside, up gentle hills which surprise with breathtaking views, by way of picturesque villages and into the shade of the beechwoods. They are peaceful and reassuring.

I have no hesitation in repeating that a walk may be made or marred by the shoes one wears. Strong shoes, even on a dry day, ensure a comfortable outing.

The Countryside Code is law to all who love the country-side. Naturally picnics give pleasure, but litter does not. Gates are there for a purpose and should be shut behind you, and wild flowers live longer growing than picked.

We, as a family, have enjoyed every one of these walks, and I hope that you will too.

V. B. BURDEN 1974

Abbreviations

P.F.	Public Footpath
P.F. & B.	Public Footpath and Bridleway
W.A.	White Arrow

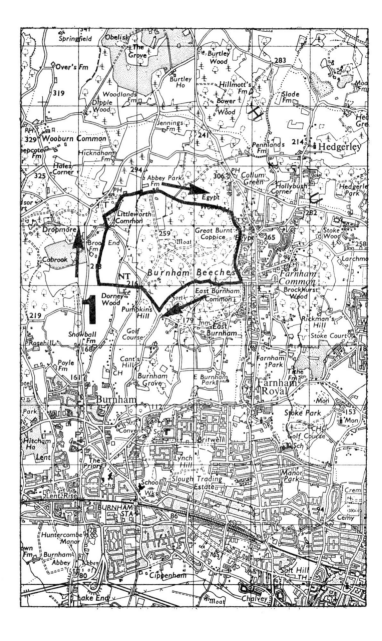

Burnham Beeches

Through the Beeches to Egypt Woods
5 miles

BURNHAM BEECHES, beauty spot and tourist attraction, is one of the best known areas of Buckinghamshire. As a centre for walking it has many advantages. Parking is straightforward, and if you do not want the bother of carrying lunch with you, this is no ordinary car park and a picnic nearby can be delightful. The short stretches of road encountered on this particular route are all quiet, rural ways. No hills, few stiles, well used and usually dry paths, and two country pubs all help in recommending it for any day of the year. Yet, oddly enough, despite all this it remains one of the easiest of places in which to lose one's way. But if you follow this suggested route, you should not go astray. So numerous are the tracks and paths that, to avoid a constant repetition of reminders not to be lured away by turnings off, the given directions keep to the main paths unless otherwise stated.

To locate the car park from the A.355 at Farnham Common go down the short length of Beeches Road, as signposted to Burnham Beeches, and at end cross road to Lord Mayor's Drive, and there facing you is the pleasantly situated car park. The walk sets off straight along Lord Mayor's Drive, where at first you see silver birch and spurs of broom gilding the bracken, but once past a white car-barrier, the beeches take over. As the Drive divides follow the right fork which quickly joins Sir Henry Peek's Drive to become Halse Drive. Continuing forward with Drive as it moves left you will pass one or two of the famous age-old beeches. Pollarded again and again, the curtailed branches emerging from mammoth trunks have become, to borrow Lewis Carroll's phrase, 'curiouser and curiouser'. After approximately a $\frac{1}{4}$ of a mile at bottom of dip and just prior to Drive sweeping right, turn left along a wide track.

Here, to the left, an enclosure preserves trees planted some 300 years ago, but now as you go on, the straight, slender trunks of younger beech appear. Some reveal their shallow roots straddled along a mossy bank. At length, as all around the land dips and curves like a tempestuous sea, the track meets a road where turn sharp right. Rather more than a $\frac{1}{4}$ of a mile on reach a signpost where Pumpkin Hill, along which you have come, Green Park and Currier's Lane foregather. Just beyond the Currier's Lane sign, on left take the P.F. over stile and across a tree-ringed meadow. A gate and P.F. sign at its far side bring you to road, which cross to P.F. opposite and path ahead is unmistakable. Even more treetops are now outlined upon the distant horizon. On arrival at another gate go through, but disregard tempting bridleway ahead, and turn immediately right into field and follow round its right edge. You will be led into next field and a view of the brick and timbered Brook Farm away to left. But turn right and round corner of field to go on again maintaining your previous direction. At the further edge of this field path moves a pace or two to the left, through a gap and now still goes on by right edge of next field. The far side of this one merely merges into a tree-dotted meadow where turn left for a few paces. Then bear right for a step or two up to an oak. From here go past pond and with ditch and line of oaks on your right go straight up to wide gate. (Do not aim at gate marked by a red post beside large house away to left.)

Beyond wide gate is a junction of four country roads, and the way is forward past The Beech Tree and up Dorney Wood Road for only 100 yards. At this point, and just short of a cross-roads sign, go off right on to a path cutting through the Common.

This pretty path, where birch and bracken grow in harmony, emerges at The Blackwood Arms at Littleworth Common. Ignore P.F. to right beneath a cherry tree, and walk past pub and along road as it edges the Common. I always expect to see ducks, coot or at least a moorhen on the

10

pond to left, but every time we pass by the clouded water is still and quiet and there has been no sign of wildlife.

On arrival at a road junction turn right passing farm and on till you see a three-armed signpost. Here, as you discover you have just come along Boveney Wood Lane, carry straight on as indicated to Burnham Beeches. But very shortly abandon road to take P.F. by the solitary Abbey Park Cottage. Quickly guiding over stile path takes you on, surrounded at first by pastoral scenery, but once over next stile, by the familiar beeches. Known as Egypt Wood, these woodlands are said to have been so called because of the gypsies or 'Egyptians' who used to camp here. Much of the immediate land is private but just beyond a broad private track off right, go forward along right fork delving deeper into wood. Dipping down and up again it is soon bordered by a fir plantation on left and finally arrives at a group of houses, Egypt Wood Cottages, where go forward on surfaced drive to road.

Turn right along road for about a ¼ of a mile and immediately past The Old Cottage, with its single dormer window, as the road forks ignore turning right and keep straight on. Shortly crossing over The Avenue this road will take you the ½ mile or so back to Lord Mayor's Drive. Alternatively, and even more pleasantly, make your way there on the numerous paths through the beeches running more or less parallel with road.

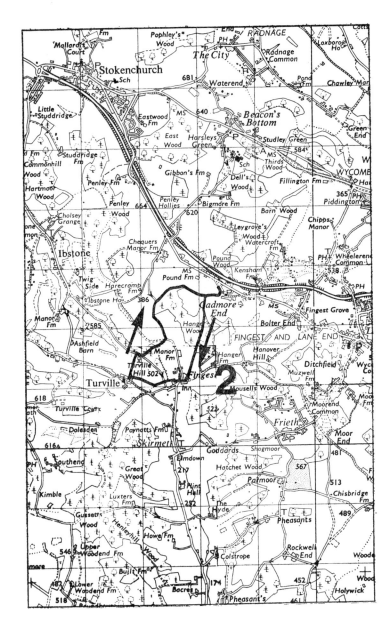

Cadmore End

Following ancient tracks to Fingest and Turville
3½ miles

ALTHOUGH this looks from the mileage as though it is rather a short walk, I would suggest that you allow at least a couple of hours for it. One reason is that it includes the fairly steep climb of Turville Hill (about 500 ft.), but the more important reason is that it touches the two rather special and very old villages of Fingest and Turville and it would be a pity not to linger and explore them en route. Both have inns at which it is a pleasure to halt awhile.

Cadmore End, once part of Fingest but now a separate parish, extends around small aprons of common, and parking is possible either opposite the school or beside the church. Set off from the bus stop by the school and go up the no through road to reach the Victorian church; its small proportions and charming little bell tower, although of no great architectural significance, fit the village. It is guarded by a group of Scots firs. Now bear right to see and follow a P.F. & B. to the left of a house called *Celeste*. At once you realise one of the pleasures of walking from these outlying villages, for immediately you are on a typical country track sheltered by thick hedgerows. After 200 yards ignore track to your right, as the one you are on bends sharp left to hurry downhill and soon offers lovely views over the valley.

On entering the woodland the track divides, so take the right fork up and into Hanger Wood, passing an individual circular green footpath sign. Keep ahead between the plantation which at first glance appears to be mostly Norway spruce, i.e. the Christmas tree. On looking more closely you will discover a fair sprinkling of larch and beech. There is also some Sitka spruce; it is distinguished by very pointed needles which have a bluish tinge. Coming from the Pacific Coast of North America it was only introduced to England about a century ago.

Go on and over a crossing track, where we were lucky enough to spot a pair of deer, and ahead till path forks once more. Do not go left, but on and down as path narrows and when it makes its exit from wood there is a fine prospect of Fingest. The unmistakable way continues down, with Turville, or Ibstone Mill as it is alternatively called, away to right, and comes to a wooden stile where go diagonally across meadow to similar stile. Beyond it go forward to pass between houses and emerge in the village of Fingest.

A visit to the Norman church with its fortress-like tower and famous saddle-back roof might be suggested here. Then the way is on past the church to reach the road junction by The Chequers. By going right till the churchyard wall ends you will find a stile ahead, by a P.F. sign, which cross. Walk along narrow path bounded by a good old flint wall, and as you re-enter woodland go sharp left thus staying by edge of trees. At a double P.F. sign cross road to go over a pair of stiles very close together. Then the track wends its way along the lower slope of the hill to meet another stile. Climb and go half left down to opposite corner of field, when Turville can be seen before you. In the corner of the field cross stile, and 50 paces on the direction is right and over another stile.

Turville, which is off to your left, is a compact little place. The centuries-old cottages cluster about the church, also of Norman origin, but it differs from the church at Fingest having a very short tower and far less formidable appearance. The picturesque Bull and Butcher inn has a pleasant garden.

When ready to continue go over stile and straight up towards the Mill. The path initially hugs the left hand side of the field, but beyond next stile changes to follow right edge of adjoining field. A rest part-way allows you to look back on the weathered roofs of Turville tucked so very neatly into the deep cleft of the hills. On gaining the top, the Mill, now a private house, is to your right. You meet a road where turn right for 30 yards only and just prior to a 'Hill' sign go left into wood. Once in Mill Hanging Wood do not be tempted by any side tracks as path descends rapidly and is soon bounded by fence to left. But as it goes sharply right abandon it by going over a couple of rustic stiles. Now a path leads to a field where walk half right to reach a short lane approaching the road by a P.F. sign and a long white gate. Turn left along road. This is not an ordinary road, but a secluded lane, more attractive than some footpaths and edged by banked hedgerows sheltering the ordinary little flowers— speedwell, Jack-in-the-hedge, vetch, windflower—which add charm to the English countryside, and deserve to be cherished and conserved.

After nearly $\frac{1}{2}$ a mile go right along P.F. & B. and as the left-hand fence ends keep forward along left edge of wood with a wire fence now right. Emerge from wood to bear right up field's right edge; then via a gate and up right edge of next field and through a similar gate. Then, with church and its bell tower now visible ahead, simply continue forward to rejoin path back to Cadmore End.

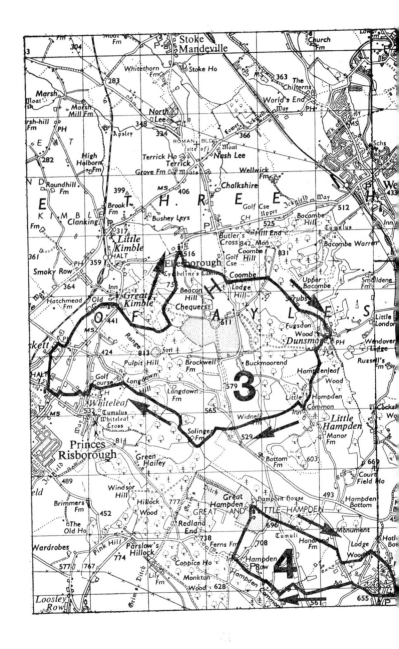

Great Kimble

Over the Chiltern Hills
10 miles

SOME of the highest of the Chiltern hills (Coombe Hill tops them all at 852 feet) rise between the Buckinghamshire towns of Wendover and Prince's Risborough. The long ridge is pinpointed by a series of historic landmarks including the fortifications of Cunobelinus, Shakespeare's Cymbeline. Pulpit Hill provides evidence of Iron-Age earthworks, and looking down upon the Risboroughs is the great chalk cross of Whyteleaf. Amidst these hills, at Chequers, contemporary politicians continue to shape the course of history. The necessary, though spasmodic uphill work of the following excursion is also rewarded by long and constantly changing views, the varying pleasures of beechwoods, lush meadows, and chalk paths scattered with wayside flowers. With hardly any road walking innumerable places will suggest themselves for an alfresco meal. It would be unfair to single out any of the several pubs passed as each has its own welcoming individuality.

The A.4010, following the course of the Upper Icknield Way, bisects the village of Great Kimble. It is from the bus stop outside Kimble church, or from the long lay-by just south of it, that the walk begins. Set off up lane as P.F. & B. sign guides, passing Pickade House left until, on seeing a metal gate left, go through and half right up field's clear path. Pay no heed to paths off, as skirting Chequers Knap right, the path reaches a wire fence and bends left around the deep cleft of Happy Valley. On coming to a stile by a wide gate, cross and go forward, slightly right, over field. At far side, turn very sharp left and with woodland now on your right continue ahead till you reach a P.F. sign at stile and white gate. Cross stile and driveway to continue along opposite path between beech trees. On leaving them the path bends left to cultivated land, edged in summer by forget-me-nots, pimpernel, cinque-foil and other modest flowers. Journeying on between a couple of wooden posts the path descends sharply by a series of steps. The surrounding slopes are one of the few remaining districts of England where the box tree grows wild. Indeed, it is beyond a very wilderness of box and yew that the site of Cymbeline's Castle is located.

After steps cease, cross a stile guiding to a clear chalk track curving round the hill. Ever-widening views of the Vale of Aylesbury accompany you, and suddenly you seem to be on a level with Ellesborough church tower. Then the path drops to a stile and looking back only the cap of Beacon Hill fills the horizon. From here the way is obviously straight across field towards the church on its hillock and the thatched cottages of Ellesborough sheltering below. A single P.F. sign marks your arrival at road, and by turning right for only 30 paces find a double one where another right turn takes you down an inviting track past a group of almshouses. But a short distance on abandon track to turn left by a double P.F. sign. The path traverses a vast field as Coombe Hill and the Boer War Monument dominate the sky-line.

When at length you reach road by a P.F. sign go right, and after 100 yards, left, as signposted up lane by the decorative Coombe Hill Farm. Once past Ellesborough Golf Club still go forward to a wooden gate, then disregarding paths left and right, climb steeply up the slopes of Coombe Hill keeping fence right. Near the top, use neither the swing gate nor a later stile right, and keep your direction to reach gate by a National Trust board. Beyond gate, ignoring road right and lane left, continue ahead along the lovely country road. By-pass two paths on left, but on reaching a double P.F. sign on right turn left and of the two paths facing you be sure to follow the right fork uphill into Scrubs Wood. At the point where it divides, ignore left fork, and find your path soon joined by another and then moving right and coming to a double P.F. sign. Turn right and the path, arriving at the hamlet of Dunsmore, develops into a road to pass The Fox inn.

Perched on a hill, Dunsmore is so tiny that to explore it is a very minor diversion, and when ready to depart go from the multiple signpost by the duck pond in the direction of Kimble. Just 60 yards on turn left over stile by a double P.F. sign to go diagonally right down field and once over next stile keep same course to further stile. Then forward by means of two more stiles to come down to P.F. sign at farm. Turn left along lane, but when wooden fence to right ends desert main path to fork half right up well defined path through Hampdenleaf Wood. At the top as six paths converge go left out of wood, and passing playing field right continue along lane to one of the most remote spots in the whole Chilterns, Little Hampden.

The Rising Sun faces you, and the tiny Norman church is a little walk down the road, but our way turns right. This is really the end of the village road, so do not follow it right into Little Hampden Manor School, but go ahead on narrower track into a copse. After 140 yards there is a gathering of five paths, so turn sharp left and passing a large W.A. on tree go forward with bracken right to quickly emerge from copse between holly bushes. Still go forward, but now by right and rutted edge of field and as a gap appears to right go through and thus along left edge of next field till in a dip a faithful old stile to left escorts you into wood. Beyond it the path, more or less adhering to right boundary of wood, reaches a spectacular hollow on left at a double W.A. Right fork is to be ignored as you go ahead down slim but unmistakable path to come to a broad crossing track, where go briefly right to stile in wood's bottom corner. And over stile carry on down left edge of field to pass the isolated Widnell Farm, and the farm road leads to a P.F. sign at main road. Cross and go forward on surfaced drive entering the Hampden Estate and returning to the deep country so typical of the area.

Half a mile on, at a small double P.F. sign, do not go left, but on to Solinger Farm. Again, at farm don't use track slightly left to wood, but walk a pace or two right to a couple of posts. Now turn left and follow edge of wood, and where field ceases go right by way of a rudimentary stile and down right field edge. Disregard broken stile off right and keep on down to metal gate at bottom of field. By turning left you will keep in line with a double fenced track to reach stile adjoining another metal gate. Cross to stile opposite and ahead again along sunken path to meet a crossing track. Continue on and after 25 yards note another Estate board—'Footpath —follow the fence.' Do just this, as path descends rapidly to a clearing in a valley. Ignoring gate right bear left on green track, attractive enough at all seasons but beautified in summer by an astonishing variety of chalk-loving flowers. Taking no heed of any tracks off go on until chimneys ahead top the shrubs and you find yourself at the secluded Plough at Cadsden. The route is past pub and left along path by a small barn where the sign is rather obscured. Rising to bend right and over stile, path continues as gardens soon come into view. Twisting left, then right, arrive at and climb a stout stile and on the other side is the golf course. Go straight over, if clear, and through kissing-gate in opposite hedge. Beyond the game has changed to cricket so go left round back of pavilion to road. Turn right down road and a few paces past end of pitch go left along path and then via a kissing-gate into meadow.

At far side by P.F. sign turn right down to road, then left for a few yards, then right down The Holloway for 50 yards. Here go left along P.F., limited by metal fencing, to a kissing-gate. After this the path ahead crosses two fields, goes through two similar gates and emerges at road by the Monks Risborough Primary School. Turn left, then right down Mill Lane. The route continues past Burton Lane left. But it would be a pity to leave the pre-Norman village of Monks Risborough without enjoying the memorable charm of the group of period cottages in Burton Lane, and paying a visit to the historic and friendly little Church of St. Dunstan tucked away behind them.

Diversion over, take the P.F. opposite the church, over stile and then forward with buildings left. A few yards from right-hand corner of field, climb stile, and then on to a visible stile ahead, and over a stream. Go diagonally left across next field, cross stile and stream, and take stile immediately on your right to go diagonally left through next field. Over further stile keep by right edge of field till at a pond you go through kissing-gate by P.F. sign. Forward once more along lane for 40 paces to road in which turn right into Askett. On arriving at main road, ignore P.F. opposite, and turn right for 100 yards to the 'Three Crowns'. Climb stile as sign directs and keep to field's right edge. Maintain your direction through fields and over two more stiles to a stream. Here go right over white stile, bear half left across field to next stile and small footpath sign. Cross driveway of the Old Grange, and way-marked stile before you and ahead again to next one. Curving gently right the path delivers you safely back to Great Kimble.

Prestwood

To Great Hampden and back
5 miles

PRESTWOOD does not immediately suggest itself as a centre for walking. But appearances are deceptive, and it is possible to quickly leave the touch of suburbia behind you and reach admirable countryside. There is an ample car park in the High Street, and the route takes you to the historic and charming village of Great Hampden, and the home of the Patriot, John Hampden.

From the car park turn left up the High Street to the Chequers and keep straight on up Honor End Lane. By-pass both Clarendon Road and Honor Wood Close, and on arriving at crossroads by Greenlands Lane walk a further 150 yards and then take P.F. (sign rather concealed) on left by Nanfans Farm. With a line of firs to right go up drive and at farm carry straight on through metal gate with farmland right. Cross meadow to stile, and over next meadow where scabious, vetch, tall hogweed and the creeping convolvulus grow. Go down into the hollow then up again to climb stile set in a large mixed hedgerow. Continue forward and slightly right down field to reach stile by P.F. sign at road.

Follow road right thus having beechwoods left for only 30 yards to turn left at a P.F. going diagonally up through the wood. White arrows guide you on and over a narrow drive, and on re-meeting same drive go with it right as it winds up amidst holly and beech. At the crest of the rise the drive bears left to houses, so go straight on through gap in holly bushes and turn left. Immediately carry on along field's edge with hedge and shrubs to the left leaving a towering lime a few paces to right, and come to a drive via an open gateway where turn right along drive. It is thickly shaded and brings you to meet a small road. Turn right past brick cottages and farm, and the way now snakes downhill and after a $\frac{1}{4}$ mile comes to a SCHOOL sign. Simply carry on ahead, ignoring roads to either side, by following line of telegraph poles as you go up through Hampden Row and past the Post Office. You will also pass the cricket ground on left and at the crossroads with Hampden Arms just off to right, go over, past signpost and up the No Through Road.

Cutting across the Common and with long cottage gardens on the right, the asphalt track soon bears left where leave it to use P.F. on right. Beginning as a mown grass track it passes stile right and widens out to soon pass through a wide gap below a massive ash. The right hand field is divided from you by a hedgerow, partially cut down and making brave efforts to re-establish itself. Meet a surfaced drive which cross and forward by means of stile (not the one to right) and along right edge of grazing land, frequented by sheep, to soon veer slightly left towards church. Note a particularly fine sweet chestnut on the way.

A kissing-gate allows you to enter churchyard and path leads beside church to emerge at drive. In the church is a poignant memorial to Hampden's first wife, Elizabeth, and a strange over-elaborate one to Hampden himself. Unfortunately, church is frequently closed. Vandalism in country churches has made it necessary for many doors to remain locked.

From the drive the Gothic roof of Hampden House is before you. We go right, but a few steps to the left will provide a view of the more impressive front of the house, once John Hampden's home. Walking along the drive one is very conscious of the admirably secluded position of house and church set in the acres of the Hampden estate. There is not another brick or stone in sight apart from the lodge at which we now arrive. At the lodge gates disregard P.F. left and road right, and go forward. A pair of Scots pine add, as these trees always do, a picturesque touch to the scene.

In only a matter of yards reach the crossroads, where go over and on as signposted to Prestwood. In just 130 yards abandon road as it bends left to walk on P.F. & B. to right, which leads, without any barrier, to follow outer edge of wood and with field right This is a lush path, bordered by bracken and wayside plants and well sheltered from the elements.

Eventually, a gate takes you out into the open and a broad track continues ahead. As you walk on through the agricultural pattern of fields a further gate, simply dividing fields, leads you on. We found an abundance of clover, white underfoot and pink in the field. Having passed Honor End Farm on left pass through gateway, and path moves on to end at gate at road and P.F. sign. Turn right for 300 yards, and then at a thatched cottage go left as a stile ushers you on to a clearly marked P.F.

The track travels into Lodge Wood, and as it quickly forks go right as waymark points. At next fork, stay on your track, ignoring all other white marks on trees, and at a crossing track still go forward as a clear arrow suggests. There is a surprising amount of undergrowth here for a beechwood. But just keep on as path winds round being untempted by any side tracks, and when eventually you see a stile off to right also disregard it. But a few yards further on at a distinct division of the track, do not use wider track off left, but keep your direction. The path, heavily canopied here and there, twists about and re-emerges in more open woodland. It then soon meets a crossing track at far boundary of wood where turn right to quickly see house right and stile ahead escorting you to road.

Simply cross the very narrow lane to be guided by P.F. opposite to go up bank and on by a slim tunnel-like way between high hedges. Shortly the houses of Prestwood appear ahead and a high stile leads you on to be bounded by the closed ranks of cedars right. On emerging in road by Moat Lane letter-box, and at a junction of roads, cross and go down Moat Lane. Continue to pass school on right and turn right down Chequers Lane. But only for 50 paces for as it bends right leave it at a No Cycling sign to turn down alleyway on left. This leads you back to the High Street where turn right for a yard or two to the car park.

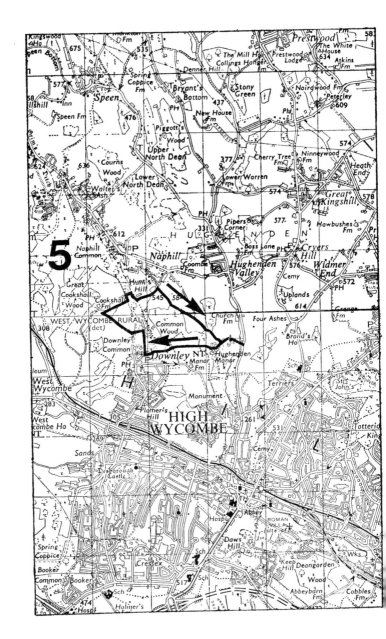

Hughenden

In Disraeli's footsteps
4 miles

HUGHENDEN MANOR, $1\frac{1}{2}$ miles north of High Wycombe, was the home of Benjamin Disraeli, Lord Beaconsfield. In the surrounding wood and park land, where he loved to walk as a relaxation after the affairs of State, there is now a pattern of public footpaths. We make use of some of the best of them on this gentle but exceedingly pleasant walk to Downley Common and back. Indeed, although there is ample allowance for parking by both the church and manor at Hughenden, you can if you wish pick the walk up from Downley where parking is also permitted.

Enter the Hughenden estate from the bus stop in Valley Road, and crossing the stream go on up the drive staying right of the church. Then, ignoring all paths off, continue through the wooden gate by the old vicarage. Just before the entrance to Hughenden Manor note the ancient sundial on the stable walling to right, and then go on between flint walls to woodland and a division of the path. Simply walk straight down through the trees, ignoring path right, for 80 yards where keep to left fork going ahead with main track. Having made a short, steep descent arrive at a fenced path, bordered by meadows and with a lovely view, which leads on into woodland again. Here go straight forward, disregarding left fork, and follow the sheltered and peaceful way, edged by willow and beech, for 300 yards to a gathering of paths. There is a yellow hydrant sign on an oak to act as landmark. Go past it and despite all tracks off maintain your direction for another 250 yards to a blue-gated electricity sub-station. Turn right up the flinty road, passing Downley Methodist Church, then cottages, left, and walk directly over the common by means of a grass ride to reach a pair of adjacent telegraph poles, one doing duty as a lamp-post. Still go ahead with houses on the right, to arrive at a bus stop where turn left along road for 150 yards to the next bus stop at which turn right as P.F. guides.

Once through the kissing-gate go along meadow edge (two brick and flint cottages right) to another kissing-gate. Now go ahead by right edge of field protected by a trim thorn hedge right. Soon the golden ball of West Wycombe church appears topping one of the wooded and rolling slopes away to your left. On reaching a long, low stile the way is still ahead, as white arrow on beech confirms, for about 100 yards down to a crossing track where, faced by a choice of paths, turn sharp right up the valley. The path winds amidst the beeches, where there are signs of both bluebells and foxgloves, to emerge at an ancient stile shaded by an even more ancient oak. A faint path ushers you straight across the meadow to a step-less stile. Only 12 paces on go left at the crossing path and ahead for 100 yards to pass under telegraph wires and reach a wide crossing track. Here go right to pass under wires again, and as path forks after 30 paces, bear right to join and follow a crossing track with holly hedge left, and quickly pass Rose Cottage. Keep left down main track till you come upon six short metal posts at which point ignore inviting tracks off and go left down surfaced road. By-pass P.F. right after 250 yards as wood ends on right, but a further 150 yards do go right as P.F. directs to quickly climb two stiles into a field.

All stiles from now on are white-arrowed, as were some already encountered. Walk by right field edge and via kissing-gate to field adjoining, right edge again, over stile then right edge of further field. A few yards on woodland develops to right, and a stile escorts you into a field having a group of trees in a dip to left. At field's far side turn left beside fence to right and arrive at another stile. Cross into meadow and go right. A line of trees darkens the horizon to your left. Stay by hedge to end of meadow where do not use stile facing you, but bear left for 70 paces to obvious stile in the meadow's far corner.

From here a clear path takes you down to emerge from the wood with magnificent views of rolling country across the valley to your left. Merely follow path winding down to a stile by the white Park Cottage, and a step or two on is the driveway to Hughenden Manor.

The walk, not being a very long one, may allow you time to visit Disraeli's home and the terraced gardens.

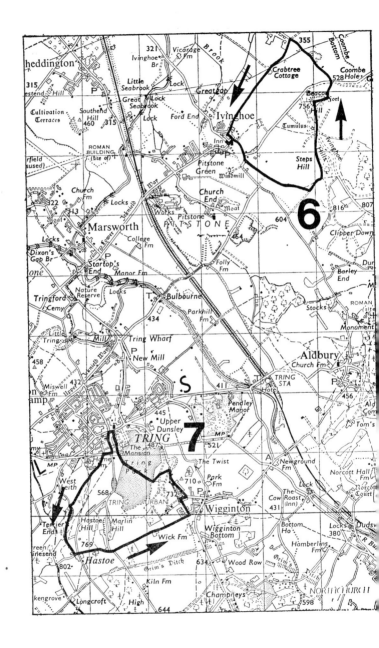

Ivinghoe

The view from the Beacon
5 miles

THE Ivinghoe Hills, sometimes called the northern bastion of the Chilterns, is a spot much favoured by walkers. Rising to 811 ft. at their highest point these are exhilarating hills and the view from the top is panoramic enough to make place-spotting quite a task. We last did this walk on a cold, winter's day and thoroughly enjoyed it. On a warmer day it would be even better.

So if you care to follow in our footsteps it is the village of Ivinghoe which is the setting off point. Parking is possible in Station Road or by the church and a picturesque pub marks the beginning and, of course, the end of the walk. From the King's Head opposite the magnificent Norman church go along the road in the direction of Whipsnade. Having passed Vicarage Lane left bear right beside the church as the Pitstone Green Windmill comes into sight away to the right. Just 150 yards beyond the church you will note a left hand turn to Dunstable; by-pass it, but a further 50 yards on there is a Public Footpath also on the left. This is the path to follow, passing first a bungalow then a little orchard before it gives way to open fields. More extensive pastureland spreads out towards the Beacon.

Continue ahead taking no heed of grass track off right, and when the left hand boundary of hedge and wire fence ceases, still follow path to a stile. Once through, round or over it, turn left along field edge and at corner go right, thus hedge and fence are still on left. Once at end of field cross stile on left, adjoining a five bar gate, then directly forward on well-defined track. These hills are protected by the National Trust

31

as the sign on far left confirms. Our route goes slowly down-hill, curving to avoid Incombe Hole, the deep hollow on your left, then going up along the brow of the hill. When almost at top of rise use wooden gate beside a wider metal one to continue forward having wire fence left. Now disregard various turnings and tracks off as you go on, and as fence retreats behind a hedge still keep on. Path is now quite broad and stay on it ignoring a stile on left.

Very quickly the Beacon itself is seen ahead. It is of interest to note that it was the Beacon, originally known as the 'hoh' or 'spur' of land of 'Ifa's people', which gave the name Ivinghoe to the village. The path dips, crosses road and a small car park and charges on up to the highest point, and with the uphill work over, you are rewarded by far-reaching views. Even amongst hills so comparatively gentle as the Chilterns there is always a sense of satisfaction on achieving the summit. Looking about you one landmark stands out immediately, that is the striking white lion, cut deeply into the greensward of the Dunstable Downs, which pinpoints Whipsnade. From the downland peak on which you stand you can gaze down over other Chiltern slopes, mostly wooded, and also see the populated Plain of Aylesbury reaching out to the horizon. Less inspiring, but regrettably obvious, are the smoking chimneys of the Pitstone Cement works.

When you are ready to leave the top turn right by the triangulation station, i.e. going east towards that solitary lion. Walk on the grass track moving gradually downward and approximately 200 yards on see a small gate and stile facing you. Do not make use of either; instead go left and speedily downhill on obvious track. As track divides just prior to road take left hand fork to emerge on road by a P.F. sign. Cross main road with care and go forward by means of minor road signposted to Ivinghoe Aston.

Stay on road for three-quarters of a mile, but just before reaching the village turn sharp left. The Beacon is now to your far left. Passing an orchard on right the wide track then bears left into a field. But here you abandon it to go forward via some concrete posts on an unmistakable bridleway. The way is now quite clear for the track goes directly back to

Ivinghoe. Travelling through fields where hedges provide shelter for wild life and for the walker, and about one and a quarter miles on arrive at a P.B. sign. The path having ceased, continue forward along the road and away from the Golf Club. At the bottom of road turn left by the tiny Rose and Crown—we noticed nest-boxes on one wall—and along Vicarage Lane back to the King's Head.

Tring

Up Hastoe Hill and on to Tring Park
4½ miles

THE historic little town of Tring, on the south eastern border of Hertfordshire, has unexpected advantages as a centre for walking. Firstly, it has an ample car park in the middle of the town and several ancient and interesting inns, notably the Rose and Crown. Secondly, in but a matter of minutes from the confinement of its narrow streets you can be in the extensive and outstandingly beautiful Tring Park. Thirdly, the Park has, as a natural complement, a friendly and very comprehensive Natural History Museum. The town is grateful to the Rothschilds for both these adornments.

The route we have chosen is approximately 4½ miles, and meets the Park on its return. Take The George in the High Street as the point of departure, and walk up Akeman Street, of Roman fame, which faces the inn. You will pass the museum at the top. It is open every afternoon and even if you by-pass it on this occasion, do note the North American catalpa trees, with their succulent looking leaves, which stand outside. Beyond the museum turn right and immediately left as signposted to Chesham. Continue to pass under bridge, and 80 yards on turn right on P.F. to Hastoe. Go up the steps, at top cross stile, turn right to follow path round edge of field. New road is now to right. Path takes you into next field to keep same direction. On meeting woodland carry on down dip for 30 yards where take a clear track on left. When, after 20 yards, it divides take right downhill fork, and soon, the pastureland of the Vale of Aylesbury stretches out to your right, and woodland rises to left. However, ignore paths off into wood and on reaching a wide, flinty crossing track turn left. Climbing between steep banks you will pass Hastoe Grove at the top and emerge at road.

Turn left for a couple of steps then abandon main road as it bends left and go down lesser road before you with farm buildings right. In summer there are usually martins and swallows circling and diving near the barns in their continuous search for insects. When this attractive little road joins a major road, cross it and continue on clear track as sign 'To Wigginton' shows. Many Hertfordshire signs have a touch of individuality about them such as this one, which shows the figure of a walker. You will soon veer left of a barn, and then carry on forward on farm track bordered by an avenue of young poplars. Then just keep on to join a road. Ignore cul-de-sac left and go straight ahead, but at next left turning called Common Field take it to pass houses and a new school. At the top go right for a few paces to main road where turn left.

The route now proceeds along road for approximately ¼ mile until you see a P.F. sign to High Street, Tring. It is this path which is going to lead you back through Tring Park. Quickly go through a kissing-gate and forward until you reach a gathering of four paths. Those going sharp left and right are not part of this walk, so follow forward right fork of remaining two, thus passing a white arrow on a beech of magnificent proportions. Travelling downhill through Park Wood you come unexpectedly to a tall, rather ugly obelisk. Strangely, it lacks an inscription, but is known locally as Nell Gwyn's Monument. There is no proof that 'sweet Nell' did actually visit or stay in Tring, but she could have done, and the legend remains.

At the obelisk turn sharp left down broad track to a stile at a metal gate. Now turn right as W.A. guides and move on as all about you there are glorious specimens of chestnut, elm and copper beech. Tring Park was inhabited in the late 19th century by zebras, emus and kangeroos brought to it by Lionel Rothschild. The museum we passed earlier on, which is now part of the British Museum's Natural History Department, originated from Lionel Rothschild's own collection of insects and his passionate interest in the whole field of natural history. It was his family's home from 1872 until the selling of the estate in 1938. Then the Hertfordshire County Council bought up much of the parkland for preservation.

Soon, having continued downhill to stile, cross, and walk up, noting The Mansion away to your right. Charles II is said to have visited the house, thus giving rise, of course, to the Nell Gwyn story. Later it was occupied by Sir William Gore, first Director of the Bank of England. On arriving at the major road, use footbridge to cross it, and on far side keep your former direction on clear fenced path to emerge in Park Street. Return to High Street by obvious P.F. before you.

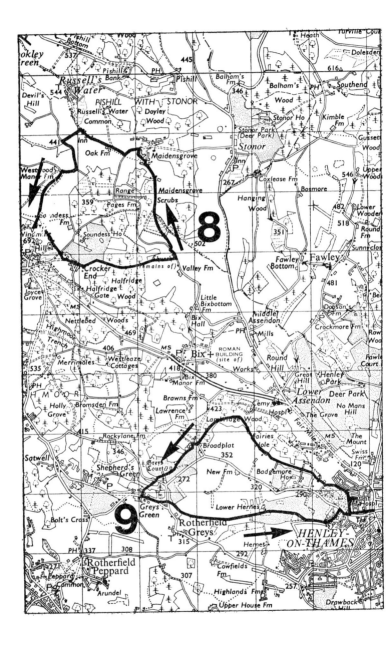

Maidensgrove

Visiting the Warburg Nature Reserve
5 miles

THE Oxfordshire hamlet of Maidensgrove, a mile west of Stonor and the B.480 is a most popular place on a summer Sunday afternoon. The wide, breezy common attracts many people who come for picnics, family games of cricket and the flying of model aircraft. This walk, of which it is the central point, departs from the common to go through country rich in bird and animal life. Flowers are plentiful along the way at almost any season and the latter part of the walk travels through the Warburg Nature Reserve. There can hardly be a place where parking is less of a problem, though should you wish, alternative parking is possible at Crocker End, near Nettlebed (where there is a pub) and the walk may be picked up there instead.

Leaving the common behind walk along the road towards Russell's Water. Shortly pass the decorative Five Horseshoes Inn and 20 yards beyond the next house on left go through a wide gap in the hedge and down the right-hand edge of a field. Almost immediately there is a superb view over a wooded valley with green pastures rising up beyond. In the corner of the field the path slips slightly right and down a steep hillside covered by low hawthorn bushes. At the foot of the hill go left along a bridleway through a small beech copse. The bridleway leaves the copse, but continue with a field to the right and a line of trees to the left.

On reaching a fork facing a large open field turn right along a track passing a meadow where cheerfully clucking hens range freely. Just 50 yards before Westwood Manor Farm, and at the edge of the field to left, go left and after a further 20 yards slightly right to enter a small wood, Little Ashes

Plantation, up a gently rising path. At the end of the wood, having followed the twisting, turning path, go over the stile and cross a field and aim at a white house that is clearly visible ahead. By the house cross a stile to carry on along grass path up to a minor road where turn left for a mere 15 yards. Then go sharp left along a narrow well-worn path between trees and across common land where wood anemones and bluebells grow. After about 150 yards join a stony road by two houses, one called *King's Legend*. Although partially concealed from view by the greenery there are ponds on either side and you may see moorhens scampering across the road from one to the other.

Follow the road between scattered houses and at a fork ignore the road off to right. After passing the entrance to Soundness House on the left carry straight on and follow a grassy track down to the cluster of houses comprising Crocker End. Turn left along the road, ignore a road branching off to the right and proceed to the end of the village. Here the road swings right down to the Carpenter's Arms, but our way is ahead passing Field House on the left, and on to a stile with a W.A. on it by The Leaze. Almost at once cross a second and newer stile into a meadow. Go straight ahead. Stay by the right hand hedge and the path brings you to the far edge of the meadow where climb stile acting as entrance to wood. At first it tends to be dark as only flickers of daylight penetrate the dense, almost eerie, plantation of yew on the left. Disregard all side tracks, and as the yews cease go over stile to continue forward. Anywhere around here there might be deer, but the best time for deer-watching, as for most wild life, is early in the morning and towards dusk.

As beech has now replaced the yew the sky has reappeared. When shortly the path divides a W.A. directs you onward and left, and again as path merges with another from the right still carry on forward. A yard or so on a W.A. confirms the route, and a little further on a break in the foliage on the right reveals a picture of Valley Farm strategically situated in a typical Chiltern 'bottom'. The aspect on your other side also soon changes as cultivated land extends to meet a rigid line of conifers. The path goes down and can be a little muddy. On reaching Bix Bottom at the foot of the hill find a rough track and turn left. To your left is a patch of waste ground, and after 150 yards and at a blue sign stating it is unsuitable for cars to continue any farther, turn right up a track marked 'Nature Reserve'.

The route now enters the Warburg Nature Reserve. Covering 247 acres it is owned by the Berks, Bucks and Oxon Naturalists' Trust (B.B.O.N.T.), was purchased in 1938 and is named after the late Dr. E. F. Warburg, a botanist of international repute who was the Trust's first Oxfordshire Vice-President.

Some of the birds breeding in this carefully protected area include woodcock, willow tit and grasshopper warbler. To see small mammals is not unusual, and some muntjac deer do frequent the Reserve. However, the Reserve is mainly noted for the fine collection of wild flowers which flourish on the chalk. If you should happen to have a dog with you please keep it well under control through the Reserve.

The track rises quickly as it travels between high hedges. These hedgerows and the heathland through which you pass next are rich with flowers in spring and summer. As a path merges from the right carry on forward; not along the wide track you are on, but by means of a lesser path sauntering through the wood on left—a small footpath sign does pinpoint it. Running parallel with the wider track, this winding path is shaded by overhanging trees and waymarked at frequent intervals. Do not stray from the top edge of the wood, which is known as Freedom Wood, and when the path emerges into the open and meets the wide track there is a view over the fields facing you.

Turn left up track, now bounded by wood to left, for about 100 yards and then bear right as a W.A. on a small tree shows. Moving beneath a further canopy of leaves this path leads you to a convergence of ways with Lodge Farm on the right. By walking straight ahead, passing a house named Ballards on right, you will return to the common at Maidensgrove.

Henley

West of the River to Greys Court
6½ miles

HENLEY, normally associated with the river, is surrounded by some of the loveliest of Chiltern countryside. The town itself is bright, busy and wears a welcoming air of permanent festivity. Approach it from Oxford by Humphrey Gainsborough's Fairmile, or from London over William Hayward's graceful bridge, and what more delightful town could there be from which to set out on a round walk.

Make your way from the station, or from one of Henley's car parks to the Town Hall which is in the Market Place. From here walk up West Street, passing the Fire Station, and at top turn right as a sign guides—'To Hop Gardens. Public Footpath to Fairmile.' On reaching a T-junction turn left for about 150 yards, then left again up an obvious path by house number 71. On meeting a fence turn right to follow path as it curves gently left up to road where again turn right.

As road reaches a stile and gates, continue ahead with golf course left and paddock right. The wide track then travels straight over the course to a metal gate into Lambridge Wood where go ahead as white arrows on trees direct. When eventually the path splits ignore W.A. to right, and follow those going left, thus keeping to left boundary of wood. They will lead you to a road where turn left for 10 yards, then right along a little road for no more than 50 yards. At this point turn left over stile marked by a black and white footpath sign, and carry on forward, with wire fence left, to a stile on left. Cross and go forward again with fence now to your right.

The way goes onward to a stile by 'Johnnie's Gate',—this walk abounds in stiles—and then up to and over a very solid one leading on to a small footpath sign near the kiosk entrance to Grey's Court.

The house, now in the care of the National Trust, was once the home of the Knollys family. Sir Felix and Lady Brunner still live here, and parts of the house are open to the public during the summer. Remnants of the walls of the original Castle of the de Greys still stand, and the wheelhouse encloses a donkey-wheel which is the largest surviving example of its kind in the country. It was in use until 1914.

The path follows the driveway with the ancient walls to your right, passes by the gabled house and adjoining farm. The driveway then goes down to the road, but just short of road the path branches half right to a stile, which climb and go over road to opposite stile.

Walk over meadow, up to next stile, and on up again between larches and young beech and the path, by way of two more stiles, brings you to Grey's Green. Walk across this pleasant green, where the sound of leather on willow is heard during the cricket season, and at road turn left for about $\frac{1}{4}$ of a mile.

On arrival at a road junction by the War Memorial keep left, as signposted to Grey's Court and Henley. After a few yards take the small road off very sharp right for 10 paces, and then away to your left see a stile which cross. Walk straight on with wire fence bounding your left, till you reach and use stile to right, turn left and still keep ahead. Soon path veers slightly right to a stile guiding you into wood. Carry on through wood to stile down to your left acting as exit from wood. Once beyond it turn sharp right and keep your direction along the hollow of this very lovely valley for about a mile.

Eventually, on coming to a belt of trees ignore tracks off to left and right, and continue ahead. When the broad track bends left to Lower Hernes farmhouse, cross the stile facing you, and still proceed ahead. These are beautiful meadows, scattered with flowers in summer, blue scabious, yellow cat's-eye, scarlet pimpernel, and peaceful at all times. A kestrel may hover overhead, or a lark rise letting forth its joyous song. The path, which is unmistakable, encounters two more stiles before it veers gently right to a smaller one leading to a lane.

Go left along lane which, as it meets the main road, you will discover is Pack and Prime Lane. The origin of the ancient track, now bounded by ivy-covered flint walls and hedges, goes back to the days when loaded pack horses travelled this way to Goring, thus avoiding the long loop of the river. It is almost the end of our walk, for by turning right at the end of the lane you will return to Henley.

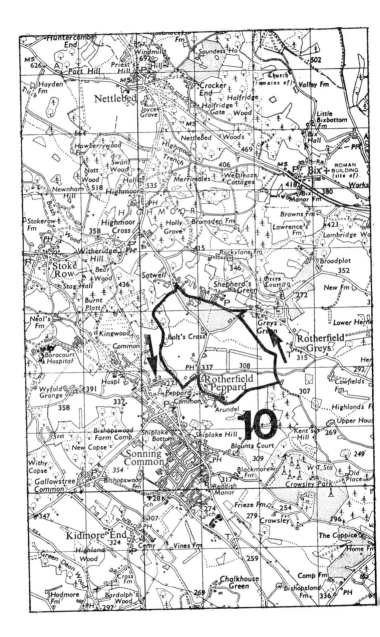

Rotherfield Peppard

Exploring Oxfordshire Lanes
4½ miles

ABOUT four miles west of Henley and bordering the A.4009 lies the attractive village of Rotherfield Peppard, the focal point for this walk. The village consists of several decorative houses dotted around the unmown turf of a broad common. The origin of the name is interesting; Rotherfield means land where cattle, *Hryther*, graze, and a French family, Pipart, once owned the land as part of the manor of Wallingford. The gentle rolling countryside is ideal for walking, and the outing now described is of some 4½ miles, starting from one pub and passing another en route. One feature, or rather non-feature, is that there are no public footpath signs to follow, but to counteract this all the paths are fortunately very clearly defined. The common provides parking space.

Start from the Nettlebed end of the village by The Dog, and with the entrance to Peppard Farm on the left walk towards the common and proceed along its left hand edge. Pass a post box and telephone kiosk, and then a small school on left and continue into a lane marked 'No Through Road'. Ignore Drays Lane off to left, and eventually reach the church in its neat churchyard. All Saints' was built in the 12th century on the site of an even earlier Saxon church, but now it is beautified by modern stained glass in its west window depicting a ship in full sail, whilst madonna lilies and passion flowers, fashioned by Mirabelle Grey from inlaid olive wood, adorn the pulpit.

Take the path which has the church to its left and a field to its right, but ignore path crossing the field. At the pretty Rectory Cottage, where path divides, yet again ignore footpath off to right and take path to left, having crossed a modern stile, into a field. We found yellowhammers much in evidence. Continue diagonally across field heading for a stile and a white sign with the request 'Please respect Game Rights Reserve.' A gentle incline faces you, and the pleasant Oxfordshire countryside stretches away to the right.

Having crossed stile bear half left down a well defined track. After 150 yards or so the main track bears right up the hill, and it is necessary to stay with it for a very short way. Then follow a small path moving off to the left leading to a newly-made stile at far left-hand corner of field. Over stile bear immediately right into another field and take a grassy path across it toward the wood. As we walked the air was alive with larks and a pair of partridges took to the wing and clattered away from us. Sadly partridge numbers are declining, possibly as a result of modern farming techniques.

Enter the wood, and follow the obvious path bounded by wire on left and passing between two rows of conifers. Ignore a track off to the right opposite a wooden gate and carry on until the path meets a small road opposite the aptly named Crosslanes Farm. Turn left down the lane which keeps wood to its left and fields right, where we saw a kestrel drop to the ground to catch some small mammal. Unlike partridges, kestrels are adapting well to man's technological world, and are just as likely to be seen hovering over the grassy banks edging a motorway. At a countrified crossroads leave the road as it swings round to the right and go across to a bridleway, where stands another white game reserve sign, and follow the bridleway between well-kept hedges. Some quarter of a mile from the junction swing left with the main track, and keep with it for a further half mile until the main road is reached. You will see the village of Rotherfield Greys away to the right. It was from this track, in the early spring, that we saw cows grazing and interestingly a few of them were draped with some form of blanket which is common enough with horses, but I had never seen cows so clad before.

At the main road turn right for 50 yards to take a left turn along another country road signposted to Shepherd's

Green. Follow road, passing a rookery high in the trees a short way along on right, for about three-quarters of a mile. Thus you will skirt Shepherd's Green and arrive at The Lamb. (Incidentally, at Shepherd's Green, opposite a sign pointing out The Green Tree, there is a path off to the left giving a short cut back to the Nettlebed-Reading road, and so to Peppard). From The Lamb turn left down to the major road, cross it, go over stile between a pair of small houses and follow grassy path narrowing as it enters a beech wood. Wrens dart through the undergrowth, silent as the summer draws on, but in the earlier months of the year their loud, sweet song belies their size. Later, as the wood broadens, continue towards its centre for some 150 yards, and there at a small, maybe muddy, clearing the path divides and the left-hand track must be followed. Just 20 yards further on disregard small path off to left, and remain on lower track. Similarly, take no heed of further two tracks joining from right, but just go straight ahead and the way narrows as the boundary of wood is reached and the path now has a hedge to left and wire fence right. Merely walk on along this same path as it encounters another, though lesser wood, and eventually meet a minor road. Turn left as this road goes uphill back to Peppard.

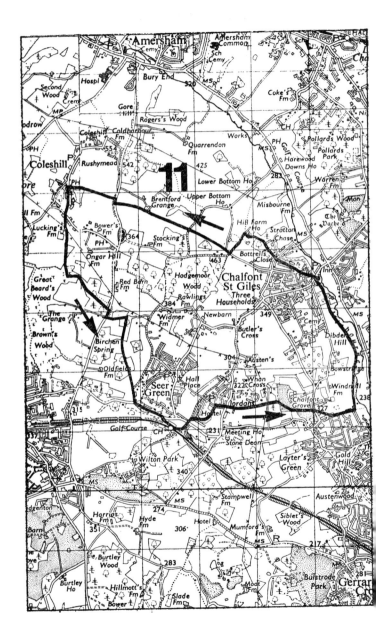

Seer Green

A journey through Quaker country
10½ miles

THIS is a good trek of over ten miles. Beginning from Seer Green it encompasses the quiet of Jordans, centre of the Society of Friends, the water meadows of the Misbourne Valley, Chalfont St. Giles, famed for its associations with Milton, and returns through Coleshill, birthplace of Edmund Waller, poet and changeable politician of the Civil War. On a more practical note there are also several places of refreshment including The Crown, and The Feathers at Chalfont (about half way) and The Red Lion at Coleshill. Waymarks and stiles invite us to explore the countryside and both are in plentiful supply. So be prepared for the stiles, and I will again only mention those waymarks, red or white, which are necessary to the directions.

Set out from the station car park at Seer Green and Jordans going down the approach to a T-junction. Cross road and go up Wilton Lane, and on it dividing go right to pass a house, Rest Harrow, and bear left up some steps. At the top turn right and as you walk along the roadway, Crutches Wood, permanently preserved as an open space through the generosity of Baron Trent of Nottingham and Henry T. Cadbury, shades you on the left. Soon fields appear on your right and you will see the Quakers' path leading to the bare, salt-impregnated timbers of the Mayflower Barn and the most visited of all the Friends' Meeting-Houses.

Curving gently left arrive at a crossing road, where go right again to pass Jordans' turfed village square. Around it is gathered the country garden suburb designed by Fred Rowntree sixty years ago. Go on to cross a major road and a stile guides you along drive. At the point where it bends right to a farmhouse, keep ahead on wire-fenced track to another stile. Beyond it a green path takes you on and over next stile to soon pass under a pylon, and a stile escorts you over a driveway and on into a meadow. Woodland borders the right and as it ends the path bears slightly right over parkland studded with magnificent specimens of cedar and pine. Then, as you keep your forward direction, the mellow dignity of Chalfont Grove appears on left, and on encountering an isolated metal gate go on to reach a holly copse, where a kissing-gate brings you to road. Cross, and continue down the alleyway—cyclists not allowed—till you meet a road where go left and still down passing Chalfont St. Peter County Infant School. At foot of the hill leave Boundary Road by going forward down a further pedestrian alleyway to a playing field. Here a red arrow on a tree directs you left to pass behind the cricket pavilion and on beyond the tennis courts to a stile.

From this point the way along the river valley is generously waymarked so just keep on ahead encountering first a kissing-gate and then, if you want to count them, six successive stiles. The path evolves as one of no fixed dimensions ambling through the natural disorder of the meadows. And you will discover that each meadow has its own individual character, and not so far away, though usually screened from sight, is the Misbourne. Rarely more than a stream, its tendency to disappear altogether at times has occasioned much speculation, but no proof, as to the cause of its temperamental behaviour.

Eventually, a hedged lane, with an old orchard rising to left, leads you forward by a stile to reach another by a house. Here, a pace or so on, see a stile to right which use and go ahead, passing maisonettes left to next stile. Beyond it go left, away from the Misbourne to pass the Church of St. Giles. If you happen to find it open it has some 14th century wall paintings among its other treasures. Go under the ancient lych-gate into Chalfont St. Giles. Walk left and Milton's Cottage is a short distance up the hill, walk right and you will have the pleasure of ducks on the village pond, but our walk goes straight forward and, with The Crown on the left, along the road so aptly called Up Corner. Ignoring a nearby P.F. sign, soon pass The Fox and Hounds. Carry on up and where the road bends left at Bottrell's Lane, leave it to go ahead along Dodd's Lane. When this quiet little road reaches a cross-road go past a P.F. sign and up Hill Farm Lane, by-passing Hunter's Moon on your left. The lane continues, not unexpectedly, to pass Hill Farm and at the top is a small but informative signpost. Taking note of its indication to Frog Hall, turn left through a wooden kissing-gate where go ahead as track (fence to left) leads you to follow the right edge of a field and emerge in road.

Go immediately right up gravelled drive and after 80 yards desert it to climb left-hand stile, waymarked, like many to follow, by a couple of small white arrows on its step. Clearly the path goes forward alongside the field to a similar stile, and on to yet another. By now a patch of woodland is away to left, and before you a panoramic view over rolling Chiltern countryside. The direction veers very slightly left over the long sloping meadow to the stile in its far left-hand corner. Beyond, carry straight on down to similar stile, and having crossed the minor road, and two successive stiles, go up left edge of field. As you breast the rise vistas of woodland complement the economic pattern of field and hedgerow. Just a dozen yards short of this field's left-hand corner be guided by stile on left (red mark) into adjoining field where turn immediately right beside its right boundary to stile as stout as the last. On its other side keep your forward direction over next field and stile, and the path edging along the next field brings you to a stile by a house.

Once over, walk across a patch of scrub and noting Brentford Grange away to your right, reach stile. Still go ahead crossing the possibly muddy approach to farm, over next stile and after 25 yards climb stile on right. Turn left and maintaining the same course along a couple of fields with adjoining stile, arrive at the A.355 Cross with care, and 40 paces to your right go down steep bank to rough stile by no more than a green stump of a P.F. sign. Beyond the way is forward over a prairie-type field again accompanied by long views, and at length pass between two stout wooden posts and over smaller field to first meet a wood and a wire fence to left, and then, crossing stile, emerge into a lane.

The lane leads to the Red Lion and the village of Coleshill, the home of Waller until he moved to Beaconsfield. In road turn left to pass the post office on the left and village pond on the right. This is Village Road, and where it becomes Windmill Road the old, now sail-less tower mill is seen to your left as you go down to meet a road junction. At this point cross Magpies Lane to a P.F. sign and follow line of the holly hedge to quickly reach a driveway, which follow for 100 paces to a pylon. Now turn left over stile into a meadow, then half-right over the turf to stile below pylon wires. Continuing down right edge of field you will have an orchard and Lucking's Farm off to your right. On arriving at a kissing-gate, unusually a new one, go through, turn left for a few steps, but do not be tempted by path into wood. Instead turn right down left edge of field.

The next landmark is a rudimentary stile by a wide gate. Cross this and after 30 yards the path veers left into wood. Winding down between the beech, your way is guided by the friendly red arrows which usher you down to a wide green crossing track. Turn left, with the well-spaced beech left and close lines of fir right. Disregarding all side-tracks, stay with the delightful path as it moves along the valley amid young pine, larch, beech and birch until you reach a P.F. & B. sign and emerge at a surfaced lay-by. Here bear right up the bank facing you to main road. Cross to visible double P.F. opposite and go forward down lane—rather muddy on our last visit. On arrival at a four-armed P.F. sign, go right through the little swing gate and the length of a young Scots pine plantation to similar gate. Now the path curves left past a double P.F. & B. sign to an ancient gate and on along right edge of field with a spinney one side and field rising up on the other. The well-defined path reaches another swing gate into a wood, and runs along the left edge, soon to pass another quadruple sign. Despite its varying attractions, still keep ahead along the bridleway, now a broad ride between woodland to a gate and double P.F. & B. sign. Here take a pace or two to your right, then forward again along right edge of field to emerge through swing gates to P.F. & B. at road. In road turn right down Bottom Lane to road junction where turn left and by-passing all turnings off, stay with road back to Seer Green Station.

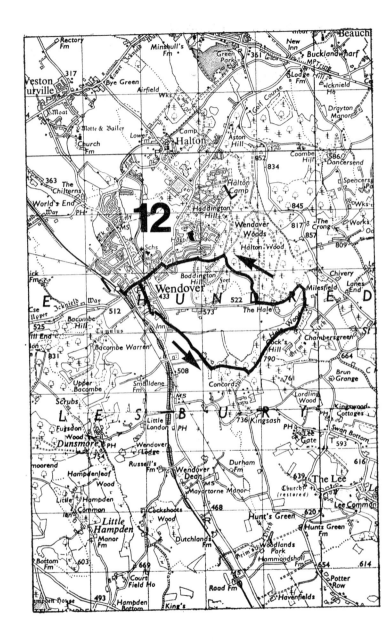

Wendover

Climbing up to Boddington Banks
6 miles

THE route I am about to detail can easily be walked in between two and two and a half hours, but as a more leisurely excursion it can be very rewarding. There are several suitable picnic spots, and almost at the end the walk does encounter one officially designated Picnic Place. Wendover, having both a station and an excellent car park by the library, about half-way down the High Street, is an ideal centre for round walks.

Starting from Wendover Station turn left past The Shoulder of Mutton and go right down the High Street to stop just before the Clock Tower and turn right past a railing opposite The Old Town House. With the Victorian school building on your left, follow firm path and continue as path winds round beside a swiftly flowing stream. Some lovely gardens edge the stream and the path actually goes through one of them and on to bend right by Sluice Cottage. Immediately beyond Rope Walk Meadow on right a P.F. sign directs you forward to reach the Church of St. Mary.

Now turn left along road by Wendover House School, originally the Manor House, to arrive at a T-junction. Cross road and go forward up No Through Road. A letter-box marked Wellhead is on the left. As road, really a lane, divides, keep ahead. Unusually high hedgerows act as an efficient windbreak and are a veritable treasure trove for the naturalist. There is a steady ascent to a farm, where carry on to pass the gates of Boswells on left. A further 200 yards on ignore left turning, but after a further 50 yards see a double white arrow on a tree as path splits. Take the broad left fork, forging straight on. Making its way first between a healthy mixed plantation the unmistakable chalk track moves into a cleared area dotted with silver birch.

Having met a small Forestry Commission hut the track narrows to climb resolutely upwards. Once up and across the quite extensive clearing meet a crossing track where turn left via wooden gate to a level path. Resisting all turnings off proceed along ridge for about a mile. And a very fair mile it is, bordered by low shrubs and flowers and high enough to provide views which emphasise Wendover's favourable situation at the end of the long Misbourne Valley. Some way along the view is screened by conifers and eventually you reach a P.F. sign. Go through gate alongside to road by the Uphill Farm Estate.

Should you wish to curtail the walk you can turn left here to follow the road back to Wendover. Otherwise cross, walk 12 paces right and take P.F. on left. Be guided by path through Wendover Woods as after 300 yards it moves downhill and beech trees thin out to reveal an open meadow left. A break in the foliage frames Hale Farm enfolded in a dip in the hills. Bending left, path skirts the meadow to reach a crossing track. Join it by going left and downhill. Very quickly you meet a second one. Still go on down between high banks with the slender beech stirring gently in the breeze.

Now the farm we viewed from higher up appears on left. And continuing you emerge from the wood to walk over grass again as you approach a road by a P.F. sign. Turn right and 250 yards on take a Forestry Commission road No. 4 with house on right and a broad field spreading away to the left. Once again you have the option of taking the road directly back into Wendover from this point, or keeping with our route which is the Forestry Commission road.

When this road, or broadway, splits, almost immediately use left fork. Ascending gradually you may observe a small badger gate in the wire fence on the right, and you will pass through a rather larger gate just prior to track dividing again. Ignore the turning to right and keep on the exceptionally broad track. Stay with it all the time taking no heed of any turnings off on either side.

The ascent is slow but eventually it reaches Boddington Banks Picnic Place. A variety of rides converge on the pleasant open expanse, and to the left is a Forestry Commission Board offering various items of information These include an explanation of the signs in current use, and two walks evocatively described as Shepherd's Stroll and Daniel's Trudge.

When ready to move on go left by board to pass a wooden hut bearing a complicated T.V. aerial on left, and walk through gap by a wooden barrier. A mere 40 yards on, branch right and down by means of an appreciably slimmer path. The way is steep so beware of slipping. At the bottom cross wide crossing track, and go through fence-cum-stile and still down to a meeting of paths. Here turn left, not on the path which appears to return to the wood, but along the wide cinder track. If you catch glimpses of the children's playground on right you are going the correct way! On arrival at road go forward, and at a turning by a letter-box (Colet Road) go down it to join main road. Turn left to return to Wendover.